# The Journey Begins

# The Journey Begins

*Russell S. Hill*

Published by Infinite Mind Publishing

**Printed in the United States of America**

More information on the "Law of Attraction" can be found at www.secretofallages.com.

CR

*Dedicated to all who seek the Truth*

CR

# Contents

# *Preface*

R evealed within these pages is the greatest
secret never told. You are about to be
introduced to a process that will radically alter
your life forever.

You will learn techniques for creating sacred space.
Abundance consciousness will flow into your life as
you expose deep seated errors of critical thinking. You
will be empowered to live the life of which you have
always dreamed.

Uncover the hidden fears that have been holding you
back from achieving all that you desire. Learn how

to free your mind of negative, destructive thoughts.

Your mind will generate new levels of excitement as you reveal a life full of potential. Discover precise mental techniques for creating the experience you choose.

Your innermost desires will manifest in your life as you embark upon a journey of passion; rediscovering the excitement and enthusiasm for life you had as a child. You will learn to look upon life as a gift of the Divine, savoring each precious moment as the treasure it is.

The exercises, meditations and visualizations presented in this course of study will grant you access to a life of mental mastery.

You will break free of the chains that have shackled your mind, unlocking the hidden mysteries of your mind. You will gain unprecedented access to an inner strength you have never known as you become the blessed co-creator you were meant to be.

This is a journey of Mind, Body and Spirit.

I commend you for having the strength to take the next step in your spiritual evolution.

Russell Hill
Master Teacher

"As you think,
so shall you be."

# *Abundance Consciousness*

Y ou were born to lead a full, complete and
joyous life. Your destiny is to bless the world
with your gifts and talents so graciously
bestowed upon you by Infinite Intelligence.
Abundance is your natural heritage.

To understand abundance consciousness you must first
discover the meaning of abundance. The dictionary
describes abundance as:

> 1) A great and plentiful amount
> 2) Fullness to overflowing
> 3) Affluence, wealth

Abundance in its truest sense is not the accumulation or possession of material wealth; it is a state of mind. Abundance is to live in the flow of the Divine, to partake of the boundless nature of the Universe. Abundance consciousness is a knowing that you are a co-creator with the Divine.

True abundance is living in faith, resting in the knowledge that your every need is provided for, that the Universe is a generous benefactor.

Ancient cultures referred to this Divine Knowing as *Gnosis*, an undeniable connection to ALL THAT IS, a true understanding of your innermost being that reaches far beyond what mere words can convey. It is nothing less than an awakening of the mind.

Everything the Universe IS and everything it IS NOT is locked within your MIND. Your Mind is the Progenitor of Life, the fountainhead of existence. You are the ONE true heir to ALL THAT IS.

Abundance and prosperity flow as a result of your knowing the truth of who you are. Why would the Universe deny anything to itself? It would not. Everything you desire is not only possible, but very much achievable.

When your mind recognizes and accepts the fact that you

are connected to everything, all events and occurrences, then you cannot but live a life of abundance.

There is no possibility of living a life of lack and limitation once you know, accept and live the Greatest Secret Ever Told.

"The world is but a canvas to the imagination."

# Law of Attraction

There exists within the Universe immutable laws of nature. All life exists because of the natural balance created by the interaction of Universal Laws. ALL THAT IS exists as a result of what you might call the Cosmic Dance, the interplay of universal forces acting upon each other.

One central theme to the Cosmic Dance is the Science of Mind. Your mind is the source of all creative thought. All experience is the natural outcome of your thoughts being projected into the physical universe.

The Law of Attraction works upon the universal

principle that "Like attracts Like". All physical matter is fundamentally a mass of energy vibrating at a specific speed and frequency. Everything that you perceive, no matter the form, is nothing more than energy in motion. Energy will always seek out and attract other forms of energy that are similar in quality and vibration.

The Universe works by Divine Order. All forms of life are either moving into one form of expression or out of another. Life is active; nothing remains stagnant.

You are the Life Principle in action; your mind is constantly active. You are in essence an experience creating machine. The universe, by default, will always match your thoughts to your experience.

Think about love and you will find love; love will be drawn to you like a magnet. Picture yourself as being healthy in your mind and you will experience health. You may also feel and experience an overall sense of vitality and well-being.

The thoughts and images that you project from your mind are the experiences that will manifest in your life. Your thoughts attract energy vortexes that are similar in quality and vibration.

The Law of Attraction is a powerful tool and a prevailing force in your life. The undeniable reality is that you use it everyday. You will have tapped into a great secret when you learn to use the Law of Attraction to your advantage.

You are a co-creator with the Divine.

"Vision is the art of
seeing the invisible."

# Law of Increase

Harnessing the creative power of the mind gives you the ability to manifest anything you desire. There is a divine law which governs your ability to expand that which you have created; it is called the "Law of Increase". The Law of Increase builds upon that which you have already manifested in your life.

At first glance you could say the Law of Attraction and the Law of Increase are identical; however, there is a subtle difference. The Law of Attraction draws things and experiences to you based upon your internal subconscious thoughts; the Law of Increase will grow and magnify any thought you dwell upon or give special attention.

There is one absolute aspect of the "Law of Increase" which can never be violated and that is "Nature never takes away in order to give". Simply stated, when you create you are not taking away from someone else. The unlimited nature of the universe supports this; the more you create, the richer everyone's life becomes.

Understanding this principle leads to great insight. You can have everything you desire and know for certain that all of your brothers and sisters will also share in the inexhaustible wealth the Universe has to offer.

Abundance consciousness is really very simple. You will be amazed at the effect on your life when you learn and live a few simple concepts.

1) Mind is the creator of all
2) The Universe is unlimited
3) Thoughts attract and create
4) All possibility exists

You and the Universe are one cohesive unit working together to accomplish a single solitary goal. Your purpose for existence is to experience your unlimited nature. This was how the Creator designed the game from the beginning.

"To succeed, we must first believe that we can."

# Quick Synopsis

**B**efore you proceed take some time to contemplate the magnitude of what you have learned.

Here is a quick summary:

- The Law of Abundance is the realization that there is always enough and always a way to make anything you desire happen.
- The Law of Attraction brings into your experience and awareness the things that you think about.
- The Law of Increase expands and grows anything or experience that you focus your attention on.

In order to achieve Prosperity Consciousness you must understand two principles:

1) Law of Attraction
2) Law of Increase

Your mind and subconscious mind create experiences in your life based upon the internal dialogue that directs your life, and like attracts like. When you have a thought of peace, compassion and love, you attract peace, compassion and love into your life. The same is true for the opposite.

That which you give attention to is magnified and increased. When you have a thought of health, companionship, wealth or success, you experience better health, an increase in the quality of companionship, an increase in wealth and greater success. The same is true for the opposite.

There is absolutely nothing this fails to work with and there is no limit placed upon this law.

The Law of Attraction creates things and experiences based upon your internal subconscious thought; the Law of Increase will grow and magnify anything that you dwell upon or give special attention.

Using the principles of the Law of Attraction and the Law of Increase together creates a powerful dynamic. When you dedicate your mind to the daily use of these laws you will find there is no limit to what you can accomplish.

Consistency and vigilance are vital components to achieving success. Remember to use the power of your faith to safeguard and fortify your vision. Maintaining a consistent vision is the key to success.

"A journey of a thousand miles must begin with a single step."

# The Journey Begins

E very epic journey begins with an auspicious leap of faith. Your first step just happens to be mental in nature. The journey you are about to undertake is an odyssey of the mind.

Before you begin, ask yourself why you are studying this material. Do you desire a deeper understanding of who you are? Are you seeking something you find lacking in yourself?

Please be sure you are undertaking this course of action for the right reasons. Do not embark upon this journey for any reason other than a true desire for self discovery.

You cannot discover any lasting peace outside of yourself. You must rewrite your internal script, allowing that which is true to be revealed to your mind.

It is only after you accept your own innate perfection that you will be able to affect any real change in your life. The path you have chosen will lead to astounding heights.

In order for you to achieve maximum results from this course of study you will be asked to fully engage your mind, body and spirit. This process will transform your life, awakening a Divine Consciousness that has lain dormant for years.

You are the flawless creation of a loving God. You are whole, perfect and complete. Your only failure is your inability to recognize your true divine nature.

You have spent your life insisting you are little, small and insignificant. You have adopted the role of victim, believing you are unimportant in the eyes of God. You believe you have to perform like a trained monkey in order to command the love and respect of your Creator.

You have placed your faith and confidence in an insane idea. You believe in the notion that you need to prove your worthiness before you are allowed into the Divine presence. This is a great lie. A lie you have bought into;

a lie you continued to insist is true.

Is there a portion of ALL THAT IS that is not worthy of our Creators love?

In your forgetfulness you have created a false reality. Your mind has ventured into psychosis and created a scenario in which you are to be reprimanded for misconduct. You believe punishment must be imposed for the acts you have committed. You have a disturbing need to be chastised for your perceived indiscretions.

The world believes in punishment and redemption. You have willingly assumed the role of judge, jury and executioner. A life of judging and seeking retribution is no life at all; it could barely be called existence.

Is the Universe so vengeful and cruel that it has to punish the innocent?

The idea of needing to prove your worthiness could not be farther from the truth. You have never committed any act for which you need to repent. God's love is not doled out as a matter of merit. Love is unconditional or it would not be love.

Your Creator has never judged you. It is not the function of the Universe to judge. The only judgment you have ever experienced was generated by your own lack of understanding. Judgment has no purpose except to disparage and condemn. Divine beings do not engage in senseless, hurtful or meaningless activities.

Move forward in your life with the knowledge that you are the perfect creation of a loving God. The Universe does not hold the scales of justice. There is no right or wrong, there is only experience and in that experience you will learn what serves you and what does not.

Remember the golden rule, "Do unto others as you would have them do unto you."

"A relaxed mind is
a happy mind."

# Relaxation Technique

F ind a comfortable position. Maintaining a perfect posture is not your main consideration; you only want to find a position that is comfortable.

Close your eyes and take a slow deep breath in through your nose; hold the breath for a few seconds and as you exhale through your mouth relax your body. Take another breath in through your nose, hold for a few seconds and slowly exhale through your mouth. Inhale and exhale, releasing all stress and worry. Breathe in and out. In and out. Continue this pattern of breathing until you fall into a comfortable rhythm. Let your body and comfort level set the pace and length of each breath.

As you breathe in, you are energizing your body with the Eternal Life Principle. The very essence of the universe is flowing through your body. Breathe deeply; as you breathe, continue to relax your body, freeing your mind of stress and worry. Feel the lightness of your body as you breathe. Feel your natural rhythm, go with the flow.

Your body is relaxed and your mind is calm. Each breath brings you closer to your source. As you continue breathing, begin to visualize a place of beauty and serenity. Visualize some place that evokes a feeling of calm. With each breath you are filled with peace, contentment and joy.

This is your place of peace and serenity. Whenever you feel the need you can always close your eyes and visualize yourself there. As you visit within your mind remember the calm, soothing feeling of peace and joy.

"What the mind can
conceive, it can achieve."

# *Your Greatest Asset*

Your access to wealth, power, love, happiness and joy is limited only so far as your own mind sets limits. If you truly desire to experience the infinite nature of Creation, then you must acquire the mental tools to achieve such a dream.

The ability to manifest this ever-present power depends upon your ability to recognize the simple fact that the very Source of Life, Infinite Energy is contained within. Everything that was and everything that will ever be is connected through the infinite nature of Mind.

Your mind is your greatest asset. Learn to utilize your mind to its fullest potential and you will have tapped into a power of astonishing possibility. Thought is one of the most powerful forces in the Universe.

The entirety of creation came forth into being by the power of thought. All life sprang forth from the fountain-head of existence through the power of thought. Thought is energy, a pure energy that is the basis of life.

Energy is always in motion; there is not one aspect of the universe which remains idle. All of creation is in the process of becoming. The very essence of life itself, the Life Principle, is nothing more than concentrated thought. The fabric of the universe is created and projected as a result of thought vibrations.

The world within the realm of mind is governed by thought and feelings. The influence of your mind is so all-encompassing that it defies description. Your creative mind has such immense creative power that it is literally capable of creation.

Your ability to achieve success, in any endeavor, is suggestive of your internal dialogue. Your beliefs are reflected onto the world. If you believe in happiness and joy, you will experience happiness and joy.

The secret to power, achievement and success depends

upon your ability to train your mind. There is one essential secret to your inner world; you are the gatekeeper of your mind. What you believe will have an effect on what is happening.

Train your mind to seek after what is positive and affirmative; concentrate your full attention on your deepest desires. Learn to direct your thoughts with the utmost precision and you will become a master of the Science of Mind.

"Always do what you
are afraid to do."

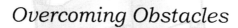

# Overcoming Obstacles

E very time you observe an event you make a judgment concerning what you have just witnessed. You do this with everything you encounter. Each new experience is fuel for the fire. You are so adept at creating judgment that you do it unconsciously.

It is these unconscious judgments that create the patterns of your subconscious thought. Your thoughts, words and deeds are an extension of your unconscious mind. You would never do or say anything you did not believe had some inherent value.

Why would you engage in any activity that was destructive or counter productive? Because some part of your unconscious mind believes it is right. You are merely acting out your internal belief system. You intrinsically believe in your unconscious actions.

Your judgment of the world is what creates obstacles for you on the road to success. With each thought you either forge a new path for adventure or you create a new hurdle for your future self to tackle. No action is inherently "good" or "bad", but your judgment makes it so.

Your actions betray the patterns you have created in your unconscious mind. Your life is ruled by whims of a sleeping tyrant.

Each judgment you create establishes a subtle pattern within your unconscious mind that you will refer to again and again. You are literally laying the foundation of your life, one brick at a time.

Your past success and failures have created patterns in your mind that automatically kick in whenever you are confronted with decisions. Your job is to uncover whether you are creating positive, life affirming pathways or building mental roadblocks that will hold you back.

How do you overcome your unconscious beliefs? You spend time replacing them with new beliefs; beliefs you can be proud to accept as your own creation.

To discover if your inner dialogue is geared toward success or failure, ask yourself the following questions:

Are your innermost thoughts supportive of your dreams?

Do you feel anything is possible?

Do you always affirm the positive while looking for the next step?

Are your own unconscious thoughts sabotaging your results even before you get going?

Do you believe you're doomed to fail?

Do you always dwell upon the negative while dreading the future?

When you start to take responsibility for your thoughts, the world around you will begin to be transformed by the power of your mind. Mind creates, that is its sole purpose.

I would be shirking my duty as a teacher if I failed to point out that as powerful as the mind is for achieving good and positive effects, your mind is also responsible for creating negative effects as well.

You must therefore be vigilant in your thought process. That is not to say you cannot ever think a negative thought, but you absolutely cannot afford to dwell on negative thoughts. Once you recognize a harmful thought has entered your mind, clear away any ill effects caused by carelessness and replace your negative thought with an affirmative statement.

*"I am a Divine being. Infinite Intelligence is my Eternal Source. The healing influences of peace, joy and harmony flow through me constantly and always. It is so.*

Become a beacon of light unto the darkness; conquer your hidden fears and rejoice in the sweet triumph over adversity.

"Your own resolution to succeed is more important than any other one thing."

# Predominant Mental Attitude

The pace and inclination of your life is a direct result of your predominant mental attitude.

Everyone has an inner dialogue, unconscious thoughts and beliefs that attract or push away everything you experience in your life. Year after year you listen to the incessant chattering of a madman: a voice which only creates self-doubt, wanting and failure. This voice is so convincing you believe certain things are beyond your ability to achieve.

Your predominant mental attitude is the unconscious force that is running your life. It is an inner dialogue that has been making decisions for you most of your life. You have unwittingly given up conscious control of your life by investing the majority of your mental power, by virtue of your beliefs, in an unconscious thought system that is running your waking life.

Do you wake up in the morning feeling alive, full of energy and ready to meet your next great adventure?

Recognizing the positives in your life is especially important when you are engulfed in dark times. You often focus so heavily on loss or what isn't going right, you can't see any of the good things that have blessed your life.

Make a conscious effort to start counting your blessings. Do it today. Spend time each day being grateful. What's important is that you open your mind and recognize even the smallest blessings. By recognizing what the Universe has already provided, you attract more blessings into your life.

When you maintain an attitude of abundance and plenty, your life seems to reflect prosperity. When you dwell on "lack" or when you entertain feelings of despair and focus your attention on "there isn't enough", conditions matching these vibrations manifest in your experience.

You need not experience the lack yourself. Being a

witness for the experience is enough to hold your fascination and affect your thought process. You simply agree with what you witnessed and therefore you formulate a belief in lack.

Do not allow yourself the luxury of self doubt! Abundance is always available to those who have the courage to step up and grab it.

When you catch yourself feeling the vibration of scarcity, focus on the millions of blades of grass in a single lawn or billions of stars in the night sky; feel and experience the wonder of a single breath, give thanks for being alive. Take time to contemplate the abundance of information available to you. This will refocus your vibration and get your energy moving in a positive direction.

Remember, you are the creator of your thoughts.

"What is a weed? A plant whose virtues have not yet been discovered."

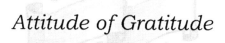

# *Attitude of Gratitude*

The fastest way to align your thoughts with Universal Intelligence is through gratitude. A grateful heart will unlock the treasure chest of the Universe. Gratitude places you smack in the middle of a super highway, speeding toward the riches of the Universe. Give praise and thanks for what you have, what you see and what you feel.

Gratitude is simply a willingness to recognize and acknowledge the value of your experience.

Gratitude and the positive effects it has on the human psyche range from a general sense of well-being to producing euphoric states of happiness. Gratitude leads to an opening of the heart. An open heart leads to an open mind, which in turn leads to the recognition of the connectedness of life. Gratitude opens doors you have never thought of before.

Recognizing the good in our life is an essential step, especially when we seem to be engulfed in dark times. How often do we focus our attention on lack or loss? It is simply too easy for us to think about, discuss and even share our bad times. We seem to get lost in our own thoughts, not seeing the forest for the trees.

I am here to tell you now, when you begin to focus on the good, miracles will begin to show up in your life. You might need to start with the small and not so obvious.

Take these for example:

- I am grateful for a bed to sleep in.
- I am grateful I woke up this morning.
- I am grateful for hot water in the morning.
- I am grateful for the food I eat and the air I breathe.

Be thankful for the small things in your life and you will be surprised at how much there is to be grateful for. Keeping a gratitude journal is an excellent way of focusing your subconscious mind on the unlimited good you experience everyday. The important key, the secret to this exercise, is that what we think about and are thankful for we bring into our life experience. When you open your mind and recognize the simple fact that Infinite Intelligence is your source for everything good and positive, you begin to receive what is good and positive. Simply stated you attract more positive effects into your life.

Find something to be genuinely grateful for and the Universe will continue to grant you more. Gratitude creates a flow of positive energy strong enough to permeate all that you think and do.

Thoughts of gratitude result in positive states of alertness, enthusiasm, being more attentive and a renewed vitality toward life. In short, it just feels good.

Start each day giving thanks for everything you have been blessed with. Get in the habit of adopting an "Attitude of Gratitude".

Be grateful for a sound mind.
Be grateful for friends, family and companionship.
Be grateful for your health and a good measure of life.
Be grateful for a strong beating heart and healthy lungs.
Be grateful for strong healthy arms and legs, so that you
  may work and play.
Be grateful you live in a country where you can voice an
opinion in relative safety.
Be grateful for...

Be grateful for all of your life experiences. Embrace with a genuine feeling of gratitude the thoughts and experiences you would label as being both "good" and "bad". Everything you experience is an opportunity for growth. Cultivating an "Attitude of Gratitude" is first and foremost a way of seeing the world in a different light.

*"Be Grateful for Simply Being"*

Another helpful exercise is to create a list of things you are grateful for. Start by writing down one item for each letter of the alphabet, an A – Z of Gratitude.

"Thought is the sculptor who can create the person you want to be."

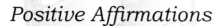

# *Positive Affirmations*

A n affirmation is simply a declaration that something is true, yet affirmative thought is more than a powerful statement intended to evoke a specific emotional response. Affirmations reflect the truth of our divine nature. You could say thay are a form of mental training for the unconscious mind.

Affirmative thought is the practice of meditating upon a specific idea in order to create subconscious patterns of thought. Affirmations instill confidence and bolster your faith so that you may access your hidden power. In short, they are the deliberate conditioning of your mind.

Positive affirmations are the mechanism by which you train your subconscious mind to access you inner resources. Your most powerful inner resource is your unconscious mind. Train your subconscious mind to project thoughts of a specific nature and you will have mastered one of the great secrets of success.

You have spent your entire life focused on negative thoughts and emotions. The average person is more likely to form a negative statement than a positive one. Negative thoughts block you from experiencing yourself as an unlimited divine being.

This is an example of a negative statement:

"I need to find success because I am failing".

This is an example of a positive statement:

"I am ready for success in my life".

Positive statements counter the effects of negative thoughts and affirm your intrinsic connection to the Divine Universe.

There is a subtle difference between creating a positive flow of energy versus reacting to a negative impulse. Having the ability to consciously generate a positive field of energy is the difference between living a life of possibility and subsisting in a life of mediocrity.

Do not fall into the trap of trying to fix something that is broken. Focusing your attention on the negative in order to overcome it will not guide you toward a positive gain. It will only lead you to dwell upon and reinforce the false ideas that appear to be in your life. Forget the illusion of lack and scarcity. Remember you are a divine being of limitless potential.

Always begin with a positive statement; a statement of power and knowing. Used properly, positive affirmations facilitate the task of rewriting the negative thoughts you hold about yourself and your life. The thoughts you entertain within your mind have a direct influence on the circumstances of your life.

Affirmative thought is similar to visualization by virtue of its creative impulse. For any affirmation to be effective it needs to be repeated often with feeling and conviction, focusing on your desire. Frequent repetition of positive statements imprints positive mental images upon your subconscious mind.

When you recognize negative thoughts of lack and limitation replace them with uplifting positive statements. Each time you successfully do this you are creating an affirmative inner dialogue. When you train yourself to automatically shift your thinking from negative patterns to positive thoughts you will gain access to an abundance of positive energy. Endless resources are yours for the asking.

Create an affirmation that resonates with your inner desire and repeat it often for a minimum of 30 days. Spend 5 – 10 minutes each morning and evening meditating on your affirmation. Repeat your affirmation as often as possible until you are reciting it at least 100 times a day. Consistency and vigilance are the keys to creating your new reality.

Here are a few thoughts to live by:

- I am wealthy, rich and successful.
- I am attractive and desirable.
- I am calm, peaceful and content.
- I am healthy, happy and full of life.
- I am surrounded by love.
- Money flows to me easily and effortlessly.
- Peace, happiness and joy are my natural state.
- I enjoy the adventure of life.
- I am loved.
- Life is fun.

Remember you are a *Divine* being capable of achieving anything you desire.

"Small opportunities are often the beginning of great enterprises."

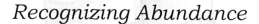

# *Recognizing Abundance*

bundance is the nature and essence of the
universe. It is the natural state of all created
beings; a by-product of their divine origin.

How often do you stop to contemplate the
profuse riches nature offers everyday? Is your first
thought a prayer of gratitude for the unlimited nature
of the universe?

Wealth is a state of mind. Learn to look for the good
and you will be amazed at how easily opportunity comes
your way.

The universe is bursting at the seems with wealth, resources and opportunity. Nature is continuously providing humanity with the necessary elements for a rich, abundant life.

To recognize your abundance you must be mindful of the vast wealth flowing to those who are ready to receive their good. Train your mind to recognize abundance in others. Celebrate the good fortune of your neighbor. The universe will reward you for recognizing the limitless nature of abundance.

Think positively; generate thoughts of happiness, health and wealth. Be ready and willing to embrace your good fortune.

What works for one person will work for another. Universal Intelligence has no bias as to when, where and who receives the plethora of abundant riches available. The universe simply wants to experience itself as an unlimited source.

The task set before you is three-fold:

1) Recognize the wealth of opportunity available.
2) Be grateful for the riches in your life and those you love.
3) Be open to receive what you truly desire and be willing to share it.

Abundance, of itself, will not flow to you from nowhere. You must first create a conscious awareness of the Law of Abundance and set your intention to experience your highest and greatest good. By generating specific thoughts of prosperity you will create an energy field that will cause the materialization of abundance through the natural laws of transference.

When you develop an awareness of the wealth of opportunity that is available, your life and the world around you will begin to transform.

"Your sacred space is where you can find yourself again and again."

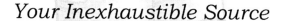

# *Your Inexhaustible Source*

T he greatest force ever to be established is Universal Mind. Everything that is, will be or ever has been is connected to the Universal Infinite Mind.

The essence of ALL THAT IS exists within the Universal Mind. All of creation is a manifestation of this One True Power. The spirit of mind inhabits everything at its core and is the very being of all things. It is present in minerals, vegetables and animals. Reaching its highest development, it is present in human kind.

You are an integral part of the vast and glorious universe.

There is no part of creation you are not intimately connected to.

Universal Mind corresponds not only to intelligence, but to substance as well. The very substance of life is brought together by the power of thought vibrations. Your inexhaustible source lies in the creative force of thought.

Creation occurs on the mental plane; it is a spiritual manifestation that is projected into the world of form. When you understand this truth, the power of thought becomes a powerful tool for the expression of your creative mind.

Tap into and release the power your unconscious mind holds and you will wield the mighty Keys to Creation. Harnessing the creative power of your mind grants you the ability to manifest anything you desire.

Embrace the source of your inner power. Take a moment to contemplate the magnitude of the Universal Mind. Set aside a portion of your day to appreciate and understand the limitless potential of your creative mind.

Begin each day connecting with your Infinite Source. Simply relax, take a few deep breaths, allowing the truth of who you are to flow into your mind and repeat the following phrase:

*"I am one with Infinite Intelligence. I have always been and will always be One with my Source and supply. My mind is filled with Divine ideas. Every day I am presented with opportunities to grow and expand. All that I need is available to me now in this moment. I am powerful and creative. I live each moment as a gift of the Divine. I am eternally grateful for the goodness I enjoy. Thank you. It is so."*

"Let us be silent, that we may hear the whispers of the gods."

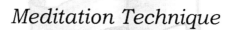

# Meditation Technique

**M**editation is simply a resting of the mind from the ceaseless chatter of your everyday activity. When you meditate you open a channel to the Divine, allowing you to hear the still, small voice that resides within.

Meditation is the path you must travel to reach the realm of the Divine. In the truest sense the Universe is omnipresent. There is not a single moment when you are outside the presence of the Divine. It is not possible for you to separate yourself from the Divine.

In each moment ALL THAT IS occurs everywhere

simultaneously. Every thought, word and deed is a reflection of the Divine Universe. It is a lack of understanding that keeps your unconscious mind from comprehending this subtle truth.

Meditation facilitates your awakening; it opens the doorway to the Divine. The practice of meditation calms the mind aiding in communion with the Divine. During meditation the truth flows freely into your mind without the hindrance of your outer senses. Universal truth is free of form or substance. It just Is.

You should begin your meditation at a time and place that is free from distraction. Your first act in preparing for meditation should be to select a posture (asana) that is comfortable. The pose you select should lend itself to stillness and relaxation. Avoid complicated or uncomfortable positions.

It is ill-advised to adopt positions that restrict your blood flow as this would cause a general numbness in your extremities, lessening your meditative experience. Choosing a posture that is favorable to the flow of energy will increase the positive effects you receive. One of the greatest benefits of meditation is the unrestricted flow of "life force" (prana).

You would be prudent to limit food intake prior to your meditation. Refrain from consuming any food or drink at least one hour before each meditation session.

Relaxing with a few deep breaths to release any body stress is decidedly beneficial. There are obvious advantages to beginning your meditation sessions free from stress and worry. Clearing your mind of mental distractions creates a receptive atmosphere, greatly enhancing the effectiveness of your meditation.

Your final preparation involves stilling the mind. The mind is a powerful creative agent that never needs rest. Your mind is constantly active; it is always caught up in some thought of the past or formulating ideas and plans for the future.

One goal of meditation is to calm the mind into a relaxed and dignified state of waiting, thus allowing for a natural communion with the Divine. The most beneficial way to reach your objective is to occupy your mind with inner activities that are supportive of your goal.

Eastern mystics use a technique called simran, to quiet the mind. The practice of Simran is the silent repetition of a mantra. As you sit for meditation you silently repeat your chosen mantra until your mind forms a mental union with the essence of your thought.

When you are ready to begin your meditation, gently close your eyes and concentrate on the void. When you look into the darkness you are seeing with your inner eyes. There is no need to strain, simply focus your attention straight ahead and gaze into the darkness.

At first you may only perceive darkness, but as you continue to fix your gaze upon the void you will begin to see flashes of light. Concentrate your attention toward the middle selecting a single segment of the light. Continue to focus your attention on the light until your awareness is on nothing else.

Meditating in this manner will guide you to an experience of your inner self. With time, as you continue this practice, you will begin to see visions of spiritual realms and eventually you will receive communication and guidance from spiritual masters. Joy, peace and a lasting sense of contentment are all by-products of meditation.

With patience and consistent practice your soul will withdraw from the prison of your body to travel upon the inner spiritual planes.

"No one can make you feel inferior without your consent. Never give it."

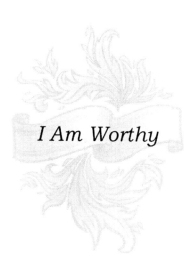

# *I Am Worthy*

Y ou are a unique expression of the Divine Mind; to insist that you are small, insignificant, unimportant and not worthy of greatness is to assume an arrogance of a colossal scale.

To doubt your worth and value in the grand scheme of life assumes the Great Architect of the Universe is capable of creating something less than perfection.

When you are ready to get real about your life and recognize your irreversible connection to the created universe, you will awaken within your mind the truth of who you are.

Take comfort in the knowledge that you are the product of a flawless, divine process. You are the handiwork of your Divine Creator. There is nothing more awe-inspiring in the entire universe than the potential of what you can become. If you grasp only one concept in this life, you could hardly be better served than to understand the following:

*You are Perfect, Whole and Complete.*

Maintaining an attitude of respect for oneself is essential if you are to grow into the divine expression you are. You are not bound by the thoughts of others. Pay no attention to the idle chatter of society. You are special in the eyes of your Creator; you are a priceless treasure.

No worldly comparison can define your worth; there is no external force that will instill a lasting sense of satisfaction and contentment. You must look within. No one can create a sense of self-worth for you. Only you are capable of recognizing the Truth that exists within.

You are an integral part of the Cosmic Dance. ALL THAT IS would be incomplete without your special function; you are a necessary component of the unified Universe. Complete unity remains elusive until your special purpose is realized.

You are an essential ingredient of the Universal ALL. Your true worth is echoed in the realization of who you are. Recognition of your true state is your saving grace.

Forsake the image of weakness, embrace your power and grasp hold of your innate potential. The world is waiting for you to claim your birthright and take your rightful place.

"The creation of a thousand forests is in one acorn."

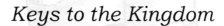

# *Keys to the Kingdom*

To awaken and empower the subconscious mind you need to merely concentrate upon the condition you desire. As the source of ALL THAT IS you hold the unconscious power of creation within your mind.

The images you hold within your mind create your life experience. There are three key elements to the outward manifestation of your desires:

1)  Your Attitude
2)  Your Feelings
3)  Your Imagination

Can you see it, feel it and believe it?

Manifesting your dreams into physical form is simply a matter of creating your desire in your mind.

Although the power of creation may lie, locked away, within your mind, the Universe will not change its modus operandi to suit your whims. The Universe will always manifest through and by the Law of Attraction. All things come into being by way of a harmonious relationship with Infinite Intelligence.

When you have mastered asking for things in a harmonious fashion in which nobody loses, then and only then, the Universe will grant everything you desire. The Universe will always grant the greatest good to the greatest number.

"Nothing happens unless first we dream."

# Visualization Technique

C lose your eyes for a minute and visualize yourself in whatever setting you choose. The important thing to get is a strong visual image in your mind.

"Imagine yourself bathed in a warm, golden light. As you picture this light encompassing your entire being, start to let the golden light penetrate your outer skin. This golden light is a gift from the Universe; your entire being is energized and charged with the living essence of the Universe itself. There is nothing it does not impart to you, including everything you have ever dreamed of. All the health, wealth and joy the Universe has to offer is yours in this moment. As you soak in the blessings of the Universe you see and feel this golden light unlocking the treasure chest of your mind. You are calm and peaceful; your mind is at perfect rest. All that the Universe is now, and everything the Universe will ever become flows through you in perfect harmony and peace. Nothing is outside of you. You are a divine being, capable of the most magnificent creations. Golden light showers you with gifts beyond imagination; gifts which will manifest and unfold in your life from this day forward. You are thrilled and grateful, giving thanks to the Universe for such a splendid reward.

Repeat in your mind:
*"I am a divine being. I am one with the Universal Mind. Everything flows to and through me. It is so."*

As this golden light baths you in splendor it is stimulating your subconscious mind. All the brilliant divine messages locked within you are now being released, ready for you to make full use of them. Your body pulses with a vitality you have never known. A feeling of authority and power radiates over your being. All who encounter you will recognize your potential, knowing you are a natural leader. The golden light gradually begins to fade. As you soak in every charged energy particle, you know your journey has just begun. Every moment is filled with excitement as you discover the vast riches the Universe has in store for you."

"The lips of wisdom are closed, except to the ears of Understanding."

# A Faithful Steward

Y ou have been granted access to knowledge of an astounding nature. My prayer is that you appreciate and utilize the Great Secret that has been entrusted to you.

The Universe is yours for the asking.

No longer will the truth be hidden from your mind. Let your heart sing the joyful melody of truth. The Universe is your playground. Endless wealth and potential are waiting for you.

You have been given stewardship over an awesome

power. Do not waste or squander the wealth of possibility you have been granted. Do not delay another moment.

What will your masterpiece look like?

# *About the Author*

Russell Hill is the founder of Infinite Mind Publishing.

He currently distributes his books, CD's and programs of study via his website www.secretofallages.com.

In 2004 Russell created New Day Foundation, a 501 (c)(3) non-profit charitable organization, which he currently chairs.

Russell is an accomplished artist, author, entrepreneur, life coach, mentor, mystic, poet and spiritual advisor.

Did we forget to mention he is an Aquarius?

As an author Russell Hill has put to paper the timeless Wisdom of the Ages in such titles as, "The Journey Begins", "Living the Secret", "The Power of Choice", "Affirmative Prayer", "Decoding the Secret" and "Understanding the Law of Attraction". His newest creation scheduled to be published in 2008 is titled "Prosperity for a New Millennium".

As a visionary Russell has a deep seated desire to share his wisdom, knowledge and life experiences with other intelligent life on this little planet we call home. His thirst for knowledge and truth sparked a spiritual journey that has spanned the globe.

Among his other accomplishments Russell has spent years studying meditation with a Tibetan Lama and learning the art of Surat Shabd Yoga at the feet of a living Master. His passion for meditation lead to a profound experience of truth that resulted in an awakening of his mind and an opening of his heart. Russell now serves as a channel of communication with the Source of All Life.

Russell believes our greatest treasure is our ability to receive guidance in the form of direct communication from Holy Spirit.

To contact Russell about scheduling an interview, workshop or seminar, please visit his website at www.secretofallages.com.

1970945